90 Days

A Book of Poems

F.D. Thornton

With Select Works By

Sandra Burnsed

Dedication

To those of us who were lost but are
now found.

The opinions expressed herein are solely those of the author. The poems are in their original form, all grammatical corrections and other minor edits have been made by the author.

ISBN: 9781796363357

Why 90 Days: An Introduction

Throughout my life poetry has played an important role in my life giving me an outlet to express my emotions. From being a young teenager in love, to pouring out my fears and insecurities as a mature adult. Poetry has been central in keeping my perceptions and focus clear.

Here is a collection of some 90 poems that I have written over the last few years. I wish I could present a broader collection of my work over the last forty years, but time and circumstances have caused those pieces to be lost forever.

Also, within this book are some selected works from my best friend of over forty years Sandra Burnsed. Our relationship on the surface would seem complicated if not impossible. Growing up on the banks of the Ogeechee River outside Savannah, Georgia. We spent our entire lives hovering between being brother and sister, boyfriend and girlfriend, and lifelong friends. Leaning on

one another in times of happiness and
sorrow.

Considering our history, this book wouldn't
be complete without including some of her
work.It is my hope that some of the words
in this book will resonate with your
situation. Far too often we journey through
this world feeling all alone. While I can't say
that my words hold any answers, I can say I
empathize and that I understand.

                                    F. D. Thornton

Our Song

Laying here watching the minutes on the
clock turn, I try to find the right words to
put down.

Memories of years passed, stolen by time

Ticking away till the sunrise

The first glimpse of the sun shining and
rising makes me smile in my heart

Because you were my first thought knowing
we made it another day

To dream, to love, to escape

To a place where our memories keep us
alive and make life worth living another
day.

Things we share, the hurt and pain,
happiness and joy

Though not shared together in reality, but
shared through a bond that will never die

So keep the dream real, keep the love strong

Because no one can take that away as long as the sun will rise

Our song speaking the truth only we can understand, our hearts will never break, our promise we share

"When I was down you were my clown

Right from the start I gave you my heart

Oh, I gave you my heart"

So with this being said our song stands true

No matter what it takes we make each other's dreams come true

Sandra Burnsed

Two Stars

Two bright shining stars in the darkest

They fell in love but could only love from a
far

Because around them are world's that
depended on them

So they do their jobs doing what sun's do

While their hearts long to be as one

Obligations and commitments keep us away

Rather by inconvenience or choice

Our lives force us "to do unto others"

Long before "we do unto ourselves"

This happens to the selfless here on Earth

It would be easy to just give in to desire

But that's not how we were built

We come from a legacy who do for others

For so many depend on us

To just give in to our dreams

So here we are, the center of our world's.

Managing schedules and maintaining order

But that doesn't stop us from dreaming

So as the earth revolves around the sun

My heart revolves around you

Tell Me

Tell me your truth

Tell me your fear

Tell your joy

Show me your tears

Tell me your anger

Tell me your hate

What is our destiny

What is our fate

Tell me a story

Tell me your lies

Tell me something

Please, tell me why

Ebbs & Flows

Walking the sandy grey shores, I find a
sense of myself

Breathing in the salty air takes me to my
youth and the moments we shared

Never lost in conversation, just lost in the
moment

Waves crash along the shore, as the tide
rolls in

Out over the Atlantic, my blue/grey
mistress calls my name

Begging me to remember the secrets we
shared

As the waves gently rush in

I still dream, for the memories are but
paintings of the mind

Embedded as reminders of the pass

Of a time, of a place I will never see again

As the ocean tide ebbs and flows

Like Rain

As night falls on another rainy day

The tin roof rattles like tears from the
falling sky

Another day, another moment without you

Is like rain falling from my eyes

Distant Stars

Distant stars shine across a blacken sky

As I feel the energy of your love

But I dare not pause to think, only to feel
the atmosphere

Drinking in the beauty before me.

Freedom bound within our souls

No more, no more hidden

Long Gone

I walk through the passage

The damp smell of mold still hangs heavy

The walls stripped bare

Left to dry on their own

Still light pours through the window pane

Lighting the soul with memories long gone

Believe in You

Practical is not a word I'm particularly fond
of

Yet we carry on as practically as we can

Dreaming in reverse and needing to escape
the drudgery of the day

But duty calls and maybe in another life our
souls will meet again

Till that time dream a little dream

And look out upon the water and think of
me, as I believe in you

I am There

In the moment where dreams touch
reality... I am there

In the place where fear brushes your soul... I
am there

In those moments when no one else is
around... I am there

Don't fear and don't fret, because in those
times of silent pain... I am there

This is You

I awaken from a sweet dream, into a harsh
and cruel world

While reality has a way of letting you know
what's real

Dreams can give you escape, into a world
where life softens around the edges

Dulling the blade of truth to a point where
it doesn't cut as deep

Casual lines, a passing innuendo create the
world where we draw strength from each
other

Few knew, still fewer know, of the world
our hearts inhabit

The place we withdraw into just so we can
make it to the next dawn

Emotions, words, and images encircle our
hearts and minds

They create a palette of untapped raw
feelings, we dare not reveal to another soul

As I lay here in the dead of night, my
unconscious open and bare

Do I dare write the words, I love you

Or do I simply allow them to drift through
the darkness into my heart, that is you

Each Other's Moment

Time passes and each of us have just so much space to occupy in it. As the clock ticks, so to do the moments we have together. We clang tightly to the moments we have, yet there never seems to be enough. The obligations we face pull us in so many directions, that time becomes a cruel master.

But the moments we have are each other's moments. We pull from the cloth of time precious memories that we relive in our hearts time and time again. Till the next moment we have. So while the world spins around us, we stand in the center of one another's thoughts. Focused on nothing but ourselves and the energy it creates.

So as we go about our days, pleasing those that depend on us. Remember deep within our hearts, there lies a seed. One planted long ago with the love we created.

I Dream

Despite what I see before me I dream of
better days

Of walks by the ocean, holding you tightly
against the cold

I think of moments alone with my heart
wholly focused on what you're saying

Touching your face, kissing your lips, feeling
your breath on my shoulder as you dream

My mind is on fire, consumed by the
passion that is our truth

I'm enchanted, paranoid, and afraid all at
the same time

Worried that at any moment it will all
disappear

Taking with you my last chance at love

Till then I'll hold you tight

Never letting you out of my sight

Walk the Shore

Broken, discarded, and mistreated love has
never been kind. Yet somewhere in the
shadows of suffering, we find each other
time after time.

Decades of wondering continue to lead us
back. Through the separations, the could
haves, the should haves, still look to each
other without fear.

But beyond that, the years and near misses
have taught us this much. To appreciate
what we have, a moment, a word, a touch.

So we orbit each other's worlds peering in a
with jealous eyes. Happy for each other's
success all the while crying on the inside.

So as we move about this life, respecting
the boundaries that we abhor. We wait
patiently for the moment when we can
once again walk the shore.

Bright as the Sun

As the day fades to night, our secret love
still glows bright as the sun

With every twinkling of the stars, our heart
beats in sequence

We close our eyes and lay our heads to rest,
only to dream of being as one

Complete by the love we share and feel in
our souls

Sandra Burnsed

My Truest Self

My truest self, Is a young boy

Afraid, yet full of wonder

Tied down but questioning every rule he
ever heard.

My truest self. Is an idealistic young man

A musician, a lyricist

Passionate for sounds that no one ever
heard

My truest self, is an old man

A dreamer of thoughts, an optimist at heart

But one that now looks at life and laughs
with irony

Days in Black & White

Some days aren't meant to be pretty.
Awash in shades of color or even shades of
grey. There just meant to be black and
white, one contrast or the other. No middle
ground, no melancholy, no could have
been.

I woke up with so much potential, the sun
brightly washed with hues of blue and
white. But then the clouds of isolation and
entrapment surrounded my morning.
Taking me and it to places I don't like to
see.

Contrasting between darkness and light my
mood, muse, all stripped of beauty. Now
my mind sleeps, it sleeps to dream, to
dream and see the world once again awash
with shades of color or even shades of grey.

Three Rivers

Decades come, and decades go, and the
closest of friends can quickly become
strangers.

Moving out, moving on are but two
reasons.

Arguments and love are other reasons why
the closeness you share dies.

But for whatever reason we couldn't shake
each other.

You became the dutiful mom and I the
dutiful dad, locked in our own worlds of
pain.

Tried willingly to the ones that need us
most.

Still here we are with three rivers
separating us.

Yet we still manage to be bonded harder
than melted steel and stronger than time.

Living in very different worlds, living very
different lives.

No One Believed

Cut from damaged cloth, the old man
wallows in his stories

Impressing no one but himself for life he
chose

Will anyone cry for me, he wonders

As that ragged last breath is draw

Forever lost, casting lots for what remains

Of a life and a story, no one believed
anyway

For Me

Beneath a cypress green canvas black water
flows to the sea

But just before it reaches its destination, my
heart beats

Breathing life into me so long ago, shaping
who I am

Giving without taking, welcoming me
without condition

But how do I return after so long to that
place of refuge

The place I once called my heart, my
sanctuary, my home

Facades they fade and memories change
with the sands of time

Yet you are there older, wiser, waiting
patiently for me

Three Words

When inspiration flows, I barely take time
to breathe

The words, the images, move like a river
through my heart and soul

You inspire my thoughts, cause me to lose
sleep

Fill me with such joy, my body can barely
contain the energy

With three simple words you changed my
world. I love you

Telling the Child

I reach out, yet no one's there. Ever one's
paired up and going in their own direction.
Except me, standing alone in a dung heap of
my own choosing. I don't want to wish
away the present. But I have to ask, is this
all I have? 55 and living a lie of complete
failure, even by my own sad standards. I'd
like to say, I just didn't live up to the
potential. But was there ever any potential
to begin with?

Maybe my bullies were right, I am worthless
and flawed? The lent in my pockets speak
volumes against what I've tried to convince
myself. Trent said it best, with my empire of
dirt, what do I have but myself. Life gives no
do over's only a forward continuing line. All
I can do is walk honestly admitting to the
pain. Embracing the hurt I have and telling
the child it's okay.

For Natalee

Among the flowers she is but a small bloom

Waiting her turn to blossom onto her own

Growing gracefully from the tree of which I
am a root

Hidden among the leaves, protected from
harm

Until the time of her awakening, when she'll
become a shining flower

But for now, she is but a small bloom

Waiting to blossom onto her own

For You

Life can hand you a lot of good days, like
spending time with the grandbabies or
seeing a beautiful sunset. Then life can
hand you a lot of bad days, like having a flat
tire or waiting forever in the ER with a sick
love one. While those things can wear on
your body and spirit, maybe you'll have
enough of the good days to balance things
out.

But if you don't remember there is one who
knows your darkest moments. Who's
walked in your shoes when you were alone.
One who's held the hand of a frightened
loved one. And cleaned up the mess's
others left behind. I am your anchor in your
moment of trouble. I am the lighthouse that
brings you home. I am the wind that blows
through your memory. I am the fire that
lives in your soul.

I Was Lost

Watching the sunset, I am reminded of
where I am

Of the place I am standing

Of the moment in which I am in

To lose sight of the moment is to lose sight
of yourself

And until this moment I was lost

Little Messages

I was getting a bit worried, the last two nights I slept through the 3 o'clock hour. But tonight, didn't disappoint and here we are. It's funny how the simplest little thing can brighten your whole mood. This evening out of the blue my dearest friend sent me some notes. Now I may be taking what was sent wrong. But for decades we've always sent each other cryptic little messages

It Could Just Be

We all search for deeper meaning. To life,
for ourselves, and the purpose of it all.

But if you take a moment and step back.
Look at things from their basic design you
may discover.

It's all in how we relate to each other. How
we touch one another or maybe how your
inspiration.

...or it could just be

The Trough Is Full

It seems now when someone yells "Fire" we hardly give it a second thought. Our senses have been dulled to the cries of fool's, even as the fool runs the Asylum.

But who I'm I to judge the actions of the weak. As long as the trough is full, the swine care not who lead them to slaughter.

Are we doomed to repeat history in this information age? Or is information just window dressing, when outside the door injustice screams?

Path to Dawn

I look out into darkness of the morning

Holding tightly to small glimmer light

Impaled by a feeling of hopelessness

I question all I believed to be right

Until the awakening of my own strength

Broke the crease of the night

Love Has

Love has the ability to filter through the
noise and find the truth.

Can you hear what I'm saying?

Just A Lie

Dawn is peeking through the bedroom
window

Woke up late, according to my hours

While tragedy blossoms everywhere,
screaming at me from my screen

Yet I'm so glad I hear nothing but peace

In my corner of this quiet moment, I pray

Is it selfish to be grateful that I can only
hear the morning birds?

Is it conceited to be content with where I
am?

Are my complaints just cries of a vain man?

Can one speak of empathy while polishing
their trophies?

Can you live selflessly without pride? Is
peace an unattainable goal?

Is real compassion just a lie?

Never Watched You Sleep

I lay here at the break of dawn, a songbird
calling the sun through the window.

Half-awake and half dreaming I ask myself
the question, how do you sleep?

In the decades I've known you we've never
spent a night together.

Do you snore, sleep on your side, curl up in
a ball, or do you steal all the covers?

Funny how the little details can escape us.

*Sad that I've never been awaken by our
cries.*

*But I do dream and ask myself, what are
you doing right now?*

I've watched you put makeup on, seen you
get dressed.

Held you tightly when you're mad, but I've
never watched you sleep.

Till Sunrise

Riding the wave till sunrise

I lay my head on a pillow of love

Can you take the time to come with me?

Or must I travel this dream alone

I see blue skies on the horizon

As a gentle wind blows

Or is it my imagination feeding me lies?

As I take this train alone

Although I would prefer not

I sail out from reality

To places unknown

Break Morning

At moments like this I reach out to you.

Hoping you know it's me.

Silence, even on the best of days is cold.

So I look up for no real reason other than to
hope.

That you are the light that breaks morning.

Bringing me truth and lighting my way.

Just Walk Away

I wish to fall into the abyss

But the pills won't let me

Medicated to sustain life, is it any way to
live?

I often ask myself that

Because the fear of death isn't as strong as
it once was

And the will to fight is just lost on the feeble
minded

So what do you do?

Stand alone on this trail or just walk away

Dead End Road

Taken aback by dreams from a distant past.

I'm reminded of stories I lived and will
never see again.

Of life on a dead-end road and the smell of
black water.

Reflecting on the softness of your skin.

Dreams are just memories, reflections of
regret or desire.

Of moments we hold until the end.

Love Forbidden

The darker side slides out from the shadows

Opening up a new look that was buried
deep

Hidden from reality

Only to shine and show a love forbidden

Sandra Burnsed

Nature Paints

As morning breaks, the sun paints clouds
across the sky

Adding to the mosaic of an already
beautiful day

I walk the shores, the salt water dancing
between my toes

Dreaming of days long past, yet never far

You are my island, your waves whispering
quietly

Reminding me you are always here

So as the wind touches my cheek and the
taste of salt falls on my tongue

I dream

I wish

I long for you

Fold Your Wings

When it comes to scares, you wear yours
concealed beneath a camouflage smile.

The pain of rejection, the marks of abuse.

Haven't taken your beauty or robbed you of
your soul.

So many take and take and all you do is
give.

Rest in my arms, because you've given to
me.

Your honestly and love that show me so
much.

For faith is the key, it's what we stand on.

So rest sweet angel and fold your wings.

Knowing at the heart of it all, I love you.

So Long Ago

Love has a funny way of staking a claim on a
heart

Attracting two vulnerable souls into its cat
and mouse game

Trapping them somewhere between
ecstasy and exasperation

Till they are no longer individuals

But one soul with one beating heart

We lived this game for so long, it's hard to
recall when we were without

The thought that you were never mine

Yet here we are sailing straight on into the
sun

No map or compass to guide us

Just the love placed in our hearts, so long
ago

We Keep

If eyes are the window to the soul

Your eyes show a place of endless beauty

Of intense burning and cold hidden pain

Our lives are marked by milestones

Places long buried in our hearts

Moments we dare not share like scars
burned onto our backs.

But you opened your heart to me

Allowed to see the dark lonely track

Allowing me to open up about myself and
secrets we keep

A Million Things

A million things go on around me

but you are always in my thoughts

When I feel I can't go on

I feel you in my heart

Though the time between us is taken up by
others

Remember I love you and it's all going to be
alright

Real Life

Scares only show us where we been

They don't dictate where we are going

Our love grows each day as if it were our
last

We live, we love, we laugh

But silently tears show the truth of what lies
within

So we move one day at a time

One kiss, one touch, one life

Only we know the truth while the world
makes its judgements

One soul shared by two, that's what keeps
us going

You and me in love while no one else sees

As each second passes our hearts beat as
one

Only making us stronger holding on to what
is true

Shared for eternity

Love, the one thing they will never take
from us

So rest assure, our souls and hearts beat as
one

Truth, lies, and pain are the secrets we
share

No one understands the insanity we've
gone through

The guilt that keeps us apart

Hidden behind the lies with a smile

Living a life of love hidden behind real life

Sandra Burnsed

A Thousand Words

The turn of your head, the sparkle in your
eye

Tells me more than a thousand words could
ever say

You are my spirit guide, my muse, my
dream

All interpretation springs from the fountain
of your heart

Be free my bird, be whole my love

May the light you give spread through me
and pierce the darkness

Along the Trail

Along the trail if you look hard enough

The beauty of the world can be right under
your feet

But we often trample underfoot the ones
that love us most

With pain and betrayal

So we learn to heal

Paying attention to the little things around
us

To the voices that genuinely love us

Always There

As I look upon the water

Waves gently caress the shore

Reminding me how love flows

Your love comes in waves

Touching my heart when I need you the
most

Never overpowering, just gentle nudges

Letting me know you're always there

An Honest Moment

It's hard not to touch what shouldn't be
touched

It's hard to turn away

From the truth in your heart

Yet here we are acting as though nothing
matters

Believing we can play this game forever

Yet it only gets harder, the raw emotion,
the silence

Denying what is real to each other

Another Day

I look out over the horizon

Picking out the blue, the grey, and the
yellow of another fading sun

I breathe in the moment, then watch it pass

As another afternoon crosses into memory

You are never far from my thoughts

The clichés of love never seem to complete

Still emotions move me

As the sky dims, bringing on close of
another day.

Are You There

Are you there?

It's the question I have to ask.

As time and distance keep us away

Blame it on my insecurities

Blame it on my fears

It's what I get for falling in love

With that mischievous smile

Attention

Regaining my composer after a fall

I quickly find my place of center

Among these Titans I only crawl

Trying to look up from the splinters

In over my head I play games of tag and like

With the achieved and the grand

Only to discover with all their might

They're no better than I am

The games we play of love me and like

In the arena of social standing

Shouldn't we all be fearful and contrite

At the attention we are demanding

Back into the Sea

Exhausted I stare out over the shore line. The tide is coming in over the exposed trees that laying defenseless in its path. Thinking about this I reflect on the moment wondering who I really am. Am I a walking cliché or do I practice what I preach? Or have I just fooled myself into thinking that life somehow owns me something?

So I close my eyes and breathe in and out clearing my mind of the clutter. And what do I receive in return? Nothing, which is exactly what I need. To empty myself is an act of freedom, a response to all the junk I'd been collecting. Even now words are hard to come by to explain myself. But you know what, that's okay because sometimes words are not needed. Just your love and attention.

Find your peace and allowing your heart to rest. Free yourself of the troubles that surround you. Moments of silence are not punishment, they are moments to refill an empty vessel. Walking the shore, witnessing the gentle, relentless power of the waves can teach you so much. Like listening to the silence. To let go of what life has thrown at you and to watch the tide retreat into the sea.

Back to You

Does tomorrow ever come

Do the gray skies ever turn blue

Has my life hit its lump sum?

Will I ever be led back to you

In the transparency of existence

Are the choices we make retrograde

Or is the balance of luck resistant

To the foundation we have laid.

Dreams are for dreamers

And the clock ticks away

For those of us not counted in the
redeemers

The lives we lived so led astray

Beyond the Horizon

Look beyond the horizon, what do you see?

Nothing beyond the point or is there
something more?

For a brief shining moment my vision was
clear

The road was solid to where I wanted to be.

But then the vision changed, my Valhalla
faded

Leaving me just a cold lifeless shell.

So now I've refocused my goals, my aims,
my dreams

To walk out a new path, one of truth and
peace.

Taking into account what I truly need to be

A happy man who living his life, in the
present and breathing free

Black Box

It's like I'm sitting in a black box

Surrounded by darkness

Thick and heavy

My eyes see nothing but emptiness

My out stretched arms feel nothing but
emptiness

The darkness engulfs the light

Filling my soul with fear and dread

I cry for light, but no light comes my way

Only the tentacles of inky black

Reminding me how alone I am in this tomb.

I did not ask for this, no invitation did I send

The darkness invites itself

Despite my objections

Can you see? Can you feel? Do you care?

A black box envelops my soul.

Both Worlds

I look out over the reality that is my world.

Outside I live freely while the inside still
struggles with the reality of despair.

So which world do I turn to, which reality
should I embrace?

The truth is I have to live in both worlds.

Consumed by the good and the bad of life.

You can't embrace one while ignoring the
other.

Life is to be lived fully, honestly, and with
love.

Cannot Feel

So closely we lay together

Our skin touching, her quiet whispers in my
ear

But what is love but a familiar reflection

A commonality of need and fear

Is that all there is to the connection

A response of teamwork and the deal

Where is the fire and the passion?

The tingling of senses that used to be real

Why do I dream of one I can't touch?

Overrun by emotions long concealed.

Is life more than a shared arrangement

Between two people who cannot feel

Certain

She kissed the sky with her laughter

And touches my soul with her grace

At peace with herself she lives wholly

Under the spell of a certain kind of love

I Choose

I hold back the tears because I am strong

I give my all without asking for anything in
return

I love because I choose too

And I choose you to love

Sandra Burnsed

Dark Water

As I lay here struggling to find rest

My mind drifts back to you and to the dark
water that runs through our souls

So many have tried to tame you, but you
resisted the chains you're forced to wear

Because children of dark water cannot be
tamed by the shackles of men

The flaws other's see are the things that
make you beautiful

The things that make you who you are to
me

So why shackle an angel or dam up the
water

There's no beauty if it's not running free

The reason we can't tear ourselves away is
because we accept each other as we are

So run free dark water and flow effortlessly
to the sea

Daybreak

I await the daybreak.

In this warm tomb I created I ask, is this all
of me?

Lover's dream of better days.

But what if this is all I'll ever get?

Do I let sadness and disappointment cover
over me?

Or do I pray? Pray for daybreak.

Flakes of Gold

The taste of your skin is locked in my memory. As the seasons change and summer gives way to fall.

I'm reminded why faith put us together.

A swirling circle of light and dark that make up our world. We bring out the best in each other.

Like shining flakes of gold, trapped in dust.

Like the taste of your skin and smell of your hair. You breathe life into a dying soul.

That no amount of distance or distraction can ever take away.

For Forever

Dreams are they nothing more than
wishes?

Or are they more tangible, something you
can feel?

I like to think they can be real, if you believe
strong enough.

That they can be cherished and held on to.

So what are we, but just two sad lonely
dreamers.

With dreams we keep to ourselves.

Holding on tightly never letting go.

Waiting patiently, for the moment, for the
hour, for forever.

Hiding the Sun

We take life as it has been given

Strangers, yet companions

Friends, yet soulmates

Our bond runs deeper then mire attraction

Stronger than steel

Deeper than the bluest ocean

Across the sky the sunsets

The clouds vibrant against blue

Hiding the sun behind its vapor

Like the love I have for you

In on Waves

Today was a day of exhaustion, a day of
impatience, a day of wanting

Trying to breathe through the negative
thoughts and actions

To breathe in the salt, the chill, and the grey
Atlantic waves

Back to the beginning, to a primal age

Back where my roots touched the ground

To where not a care crosses my mind

To where all things were possible

Where life had potential and hope came in
on waves

Into the Unknown

It's said love is a fiery ember

That once it touches the soul it leaves a
mark

Our souls are scared from the remnants of
past love

Yet through it all here we are

Just two lost souls surviving as best we can

Apart, yet together, drifting into the
unknown

Saddest Love

How precious is a gift, if it can never be
touched

How valuable is love if it has to be kept
away

When love becomes an obligation

Moments are spent longing for what used
to be

The heart is selfish, when its eyes are open

And love kept apart is the saddest love of all

Nothing But

I lie here with a closed and cruel world
facing me

But I am unafraid, my season of fear has
passed

Leaving me weathered but strong

But life turns out like this if you're unwilling
to let it go

Asleep to a world gone to shit

Doomed to repeat our mistakes again and
again

So I take my hands are off the wheel willing
to let go

And who's steering this ship, you say

Nothing but the faith you put in you.

Sand Hills

I walked these sand hills like a desert, lined
with scrub oaks and tall pines

Moving between desperation and amazing
grace, shuffling along the barren line

No peace nor contentment have I found,
just endless stands of scrub oak and pine

Bending, twisting throughout this desert till
no trail I can find

What am I looking for I ask myself, as the
sun beats down my restraint

Never satisfied with the answers given, so I
keep searching for searching's sake

Tell Me A Story

Paint me a pretty picture

Tell me a story

Show me the angels that dance in your
head

In a world so dark and cruel

Hell bent on killing us all

It is you that reminds us what sanity is

So paint me a pretty picture

Tell me something I forgot

About the love, emotion, and beauty

That surrounds us all

The Same Thing

Can anything feel anymore alone than 3am

With nothing but you own thoughts to
comfort you

But it isn't difficult for me to imagine you
doing the same thing

Thinking and feeling the same thoughts

Staring out your window into the darkness
of the night

It's those thoughts that bring me comfort

Believing that one other soul is doing the
same thing

Who We Are

I consider myself a fortunate man

Because of the beauty and intelligence, you
brought into my life

Through a forest of grey lifeless trees

Lies a passion, an inconvenient truth that
cannot be denied

For love blooms where it blooms

Through the toughest of situations, through
you and through me

To create the soul

The very soul that lives within the heart of
who we are

Wrap Yourself

I'm happy I can remember.

Days with you, nights on the river, awkward
embraces.

So what has really changed.

Family, bills, lost loved ones, the thoughts
of feeling utterly alone.

Love is just a warm blanket.

It covers, it protects, it gives peace, so wrap
yourself in its warmth tonight.

Yet Flew

The burdens been lifted, I said what I
needed to say

The work day is done, and it's time to go
away

Off to my Nirvana, my place of rest

No more to bother you or make myself a
pest

To the gods of poetry, I bid a fond adieu

It's time I dream of places I have yet flew

I Think of You

When nothing seems to go right,

I think of you.

When I'm feeling lonely,

I think of you.

When I shut everyone out,

I think of you.

When I feel like giving up,

I think of you.

When I think of love,

I think of you.

When all is said and done.

I think of you.

When I feel alone,

I think of you.

YOU get me through it all.

- Sandra Burnsed

All I Know

Hands cold from the icy wind

Trapped between worlds

From dawn raising to the endless dark

I seek asylum from the voices that haunt me

From the depths of my spirit

From the depths of my soul

Hearing anger words of self-destruction

Pounding against the rooftop

Shaking the foundation of all I know

Sand

I look into your eyes and a thousand
different thoughts rush though my head.

As the waves dancing along the shore, my
thoughts shift with the sand.

Never realizing you feel the same way. We
built such a wall around each other.

More complicated and difficult to climb
then it should be.

Love is much simpler then it's made out.

Yet we dance around each as if caught in a
whirlpool.

But it's so much easier than that, if we'd
just let go.

Till Sunrise

Riding a wave till sunrise, I lay my head on a
pillow of love. Can you take the time to
come with me. Or must I travel this dream
alone?

I see blue skies on the horizon, as a gentle
wind blows. Or is just my imagination once
again feeding me lies?

I can take this train without you, although I
would prefer not. Sailing out from reality.
To points unknown to what?

So Long Ago

Love has a funny way of staking a claim on a
heart. Attracting two vulnerable souls into
it's cat and mouse game. Trapping them
somewhere between ecstasy and
exasperation. Till they can no longer be
individuals, but in tune with one heartbeat.

We lived this game for so long hard to recall
when we lived without. The notion that you
were never mine. Yet here we are sailing
straight on into the sun. With no map or
compass to guide us, just the notion that
love placed into our hearts so, so long ago.

Close My Eyes

Lost in the glare, startled by the reflection.

Life pulls out all punches to block my way.

Ghosts from my past, specters from the
future.

All throw up mirrors to remind me how
small I am.

So I close my eyes and make my way to my
destination.

Accepting who I am, and who I can be.

Home

In my world of imperfection

You are a lighthouse

A beacon that when I go astray

Light's my way home

Your Soul

You gave without taking

Yet I can't give you want you need most...

A moment for yourself

I'd love to wait on you

But you're built that way

Maybe more than anything you'd like some
simple conversation

Or better yet, I could just hold you

It's what we do best, be together

Yet it's what we've lived without for so long

Text messages and emojis cannot replace
our strolls on Tybee or rides on Clyde, Jr

Find peace my lady

Be strong as always

Remember I love you

Let your soul rest in mine

What I Can Be

Silly Milly me, I still look at the world with
envious eyes.

Despite my better angels I live a defeatist
life.

Tossed on a sea of mediocrity, I can't find
my lifeline.

Pinched between hope and what stands
before me.

So do I stand on the sand of my fear or do I
pick myself up?

Believing what I see or what I can be.

Flower Unfinished

You brighten the path that you walk.

Lighting the way for the blind to see.

Yet as strong as you are, you are as a
delicate flower in the wind.

But you don't need saving, only holding

Taking My Mind

With my eyes closed to the moment.

I ask myself nothing.

Breathing in the life I need, the life I want.

Focused on a clear image of now.

I task myself to relax.

Taking in what the heart has for me, gives
to me.

In these moments of pain.

I let go of the emotion.

That pulls me down causing pain, taking my
mind to you.

What You See

I don't really concern myself with dates or holidays. Oddly enough I often find myself living in moments. Considering my background and the chaos in which I lived, it's funny to see myself in such a calm whole place.

Frankly I'm bordering on getting sick again, if I move my head suddenly, I get dizzy. But other than that, I'm no more restless and energized than usual. But that's how my mind works, always thinking, always creating. So I stop to quiet my mind, focusing on where I am, becoming quiet.

I don't know if this is some spiritual thing. All I know is when you give your whole self to what you see. There is no limit to your creativity. So hopefully as you pause to read this story, you begin to understand. Life is just the moments we create. So don't waste too many of them. Remember to give all your focus to what you see before you. No matter how trivial, because you never know, what you might learn.

Incoherent Rhyme

Memories chase shadows while anticipation
eats dreams.

Standing in the middle trying to figure out
what it all means.

Time is a teacher, time is a thief, time is a
killer, time creates grief.

What do we see in the moment, in this hour
of the day.

In the thoughts that pass understanding, in
a life thrown away.

Between Us

You are perfect in your imperfection.

Taking two separate paths we walk parallel
lines to the same goal.

Stubborn yet brave your beauty's not
hidden by scares.

Your eyes tell the story of a love that binds.

But we continue our masquerade
entrenched by our choices.

But hearts cannot lie, to the bond between
us.

Light Dances

Light dances around me when I hear I love
you fall from your lips.

Because I know you mean what you say and
it's not just some casual phase.

Know that when I repeat those words, I feel
the same way.

Hoping your path is lighter and your
burdens less tiresome today.

Surrounds Me

Sometimes the world hits you in the gut.

With its violence and it's death.

You just want to hide away and no longer
look at the pain.

But should I bury my head in the sand?

Or should I stand in the light, saying no
more.

Instead of giving in to the darkness that
surrounds me.

Ember of Our Love

In the silence of my world I hear your pain

In the noise that surrounds you I feel your
tears

When all else is exhausted and the needles
being pushed

Remember our foundation is unshakable

The ember of our love will never die

Search for Words

I search for words

To tell you how much you mean to me

To let you know how precious each day has
become

To show how much i value the little things

But what else can I say but, I love you

Sandra Burnsed

Blue Sky & Vapor

I work to improve myself, seeking truth
which was never lost.

Trepid in stance as in life, afraid of what I'll
find.

Mystery is its nature, unfolded in its
simplicity and purpose.

I ask so little but seek so much of this affair.

Blue sky and vapor cover the glass, truth
knows no repercussion.

Strained on wire, we balance, light, dark,
hope.

Love You Back

The last few days have been a fog.

Of appointments and new medication.

But then you come along and clear my
head.

With your peace, beauty, and honest
passion.

Burning into my mind the purest sense of
yourself.

Giving of yourself all that you have.

I thank you for that and love you back.

Into Love

As my mind focuses on golden slumber, I
ask myself, what did I do today?

Did I give out a moment of compassion?

Did I express a feeling of love?

Or was I hostel to someone?

Gave out a negative thought?

Every action we take vibrates through our
circle of existence.

For some that circle is small, for other's it
encompass' the world.

The world is an unforgiving place, but we
are capable of so much better.

So instead of spreading the hate that is
thrown at us.

How about turning that vile into love.

The Secret We Keep

To discover love and lose it

Only to find it again

That means someone up there likes me

Rediscovering my angel has meant the
world to me

It has shown me that the world isn't as
cruel as thought it was

Instead it has given me hope, just as you
give me hope

That someday, somehow, we will be one

But I know you would say, we already are,
just have faith and patience

And you know you're right

But you know me the calm exterior, hides
impatience

So pray for me my love as the ember
continues to burn

Between two souls and the secret we keep

Tick Tock

Time passes quickly, especially if you're not
paying attention.

It seems like only yesterday when it was
just me and my wife.

Then along came our oldest, then a second,
third, and fourth.

Then there were diapers, potty training,
school, graduations

And now grandbabies and a son-in-law.

Yeah, if I don't watch out next thing I know.

They'll be wheeling my ass into the old
folks' home.

Through the Dawn

I feel my breath.

I focus on the things in front of me.

Time extends no more than the rising moon
and falling sun.

Seasons dictate the forewarning of
approaching rain.

As darkness consumes my glaze.

Beneath the falling stars, fear grips the last
of my shame.

Alone, alone I walk among the ghost.

Past debt. Past hope. Lasting fear.

To break through the dawn, fatigued, but
wiser.

To breathe, breathe the breath.

Of promises to me and you.

Children of the Road

To pull you out of mind is like trying to tear
away a piece of my soul.

Not that you are a burden just, just a
reminder of the man I want to be.

You remind me of cold winter walks and the
moments when life was much simpler.

Yet at the same time you cause me to look
forward to future days.

We could never seem to walk away from
each other.

Even as we live our lives and pursue dreams
in separate worlds.

But our affection has survived the otter
impossibilities.

As we forever dream of as children on the
road.

Deep Within

When I dream, and I see your face

Who knows me better then you

We keep safe each other's hearts

We know each other's deepest fears

But we don't use these secrets as weapons
of war

Like others so often do

Instead we care for them compassionately

Deep within our souls

I Think of You

When I feel I can't go on

I think of you

When I want to run away

I think of you

When I feel like giving up

I think of you

You keep me strong and make my life a
happier place

You are my rock, my shield, my best friend

You complete me

That's why I love you

Sandra Burnsed

See Where It Goes

it's been a rainy, dreary, damp day

with a lotta grey hanging like a wet blanket

i've been laying under the covers most of
the day

trying my damnedest to put two coherent
words together

normally I would us give up and watch TV

but rather it's pride, stubbornness, or
insanity

i'm still here

still typing just to see where it goes

i'd like to say I enjoy change

but to be honest I kinda like routine

i think that's the thing, a fear of the
unknown

Life is Beautiful

I had a couple of pleasant dreams

I have beautiful children and grandchildren

My neighborhood is quiet

My next-door neighbor is a church

I have a roof over my head

A beautiful garden to look at

I woke up this morning breathing and I
knew who I was

Life is beautiful

Even with all its imperfections

Life is beautiful

Quench the Flame

Sometimes the world can be such a lonely
place

So to hear your voice did me world of good

You were always a precious flower in my
garden

A wild rose that despite the thorns has a
beauty I can't resist

The years may dull the senses, but it has not
diminished the love I have for you

More than just a fantasy or a passing fling,
our hearts are inseparable

The fire burns deep within where the
embers are still red hot

And only the touch of your sweet lips can
quench the flame

A Place to Start

I have to ask myself

How lucky can one man be

To have someone like you looking after me

While you may not be next to me

You live in my heart

And isn't that the most important place to
start

Been a Long Time

It's been a long time since I held you

Or walked alone with you down our city
streets

Or falling asleep on the bus ride home

Or kissed each other goodnight under the
light of the moon

Now we're left staring up and texting each
other goodnight

We are set in our ways and lead very
different lives

Both caring for the one's we love

Doing anything we can to protect them

Yet here we are, working for the good of
others

Doing what we can to keep ourselves
together, though we are broken

If we never touch again that would be okay,
as long as I know you are happy

Never More

Haunted by a thousand mistakes

Bleeding from a million tiny cuts

I ask myself why, do I keep moving

Through a serenade of laughter, the joker
carries on

Past his prime, with nothing to show

For we all play are parts with mask firmly in
hand

Waiting for the final string to break.

Never more

Never more

Into Nothing

I feel myself falling into a hole

Buried in the dirt of my own inadequacies

Choking on my own words

Covered in the cloak of fear

I curl into a ball, retreating into nothing

No light can save me

No passion left to fill the lie

Left in a hollow void till to all the dreams
have died

Broken, burned, and stoned

I seek comfort no more

Truly Be Free

Holding on keeps me strong

A bond that can never be broken

Hidden in the shadows, scared others will see

What lies in the heart, felt deep down to the soul

Only we know how deep the love flows

Forbidden to touch, forbidden to show it

But we smile to ourselves knowing we have each other

We love unconditional, without judgement

Only to long for the day we can truly be free

Sandra Burnsed

Two

Two worlds' orbiting the same sun

Different, lonely and cold

Both needing to embrace

He stares out the window taking in the light

Wondering when it will be our turn again

Come & Goes

Life comes

Life goes

And in between are the things we do

You are the air I breathe

You are the dream I hold on too

Together

or

Apart

We are one

Disappear

To disappear

To silence the thoughts

As the pain spins around my head

In unyielding throbbing torment

Here I lay unable to shut it down

As light escapes my sight

Where it Ends

Through the ribbon of time

The mind changes

The body changes

But the heart remains

I look into the eyes of beauty and I see the
child deep within

I look into the scars and I see only the
vulnerability of love

We can't help but live in the reality of our
situations

But it hasn't stopped us from knowing

Where love begins and where it ends

That is Yours

The body is worn like an old favorite shirt

Washed out and tattered

The mind slowly slipping away

Like the waves breaking on the shore

But the heart still beats in perfect rhythm

The soul still strong, the eyes shinning
bright behind a smile

Knowing I am truly loved

Accepted as I am, mistakes and all

The years showing the aged fragile young
love once seen

Still under all the wrinkles is a lovely soul
that is yours

Sandra Burnsed

Rays of Moonlight

Moonlight pours through the bedroom
window as thoughts escape from my mind

Reaching out to wherever you are knowing
you do the same thing

A lifetime suffering can make a heart long
for substance

But after a while even the best of intentions
can turn cold

So we walk around like zombies, trapped in
a B-movie

But Karma eventually pays back what it
owes and the love you give is returned

All it takes is faith

Faith not only in yourself, but in those who
you love

So as the soft rays of moonlight play upon
your face know I am there

Age Old Question

Somewhere between lonely and confused, I
walk the shore alone

The waves rush in to my feet, taking my
footprints with them

The salty air blows across my face, but it
gives no answers

To the questions that race across my mind

Living in the limelight a solidarity man,
known yet unknown

As the sun peaks through the clouds I still
wonder

Who am I

About You

I ask myself all the time

Why?

Why, do I waste my time pursuing the
passions that I do

The only answer I can give myself is that I
have too

I have too because built within me is a
desire for honestly and truth

And those are the things I love most about
you

Shackled

Purgatory is a lonely place

It shackles the heart and hidden the light

For so long we lived where no light had ever
shown

Beaten and defeated by the by those we
loved

But we broke our shackles and abandoned
our chains

Only to discover we were not free

Becoming instead prisoners of our own
choosing

Hiding behind walls of alabaster, never
letting the world see

Those Eyes

Through hazel and green eyes, you tell me secrets no one knows

Of a world of tragedy in pain

A world of deep scares that may never heal

But I see beyond that, into a soul that still believes, still dreams, still desires

You are my beginning and my end

You stir within me the wants so long left parched and dry

You fill me the life I so desperately need

Let me drown in those eyes, the eyes of your love

All Our Own

Time carries with it the burden of change

The decades remove circumstance and
priority

Yet through this linear effect, I still see
beauty

I still see joy

I still see faith

So close your eyes and come with me

To the memories and the moments that are
all our own

Innocent Light

She began as a gentle spark, a bright
innocent light

One that I swore to protect

But storm clouds overtook the light, leaving
only a small ember

Still she kept the faith, rekindling what had
been lost

But the damage was done

So the ember remained hidden, safely
behind a lock and key

But in a moment of faith, she opened the
door

Exposing the truth which she held

That through all she faced, there still shines
that innocent light

Another Summer Storm

It's been a while since we've seen steady
rain like this

But nearly every afternoon a new storm
blows in

Stopping whatever plans you may have

The lighting frightens her as she curls up on
the bed

She never lets me get too far away

Half woman, half child I try and be strong

But the armor's rusting away

Till there's nothing left but a tarnished shell
left out too long

A Long Winding Path

It's a long winding path between reality and
dreams

The fortresses we've built are strong and
the people we've become even stronger

But there's a truth lies behind our eyes

Of the pain

Of the longing

Of the absolute fear

So we continue to dance around the flame
hoping no one will see

The ember of truth that's lies buried in a life
that deserved to be

Awaiting the Next Wave

The waves crashing, the salty air, they
remind me of the last moments we spent
alone

Hand in hand, arm in arm is the ember
faded

Just kids too foolish and restless to know
what love is

Looking beyond what was already there,
awaiting the next wave

Ash & Dust

No parades in your honor

No gift of gratitude will be shared

Only tears shed by precious few

Markers that go ignored

Row after row of granite and marble

Pews of the dead, memories forgotten

Send me to the wind

Ash and dust scattered

For memorial and memory are intended for
the heart